A Minimalist Fashion Dressing with Purpose and Style

Copyright © 2023 by Hazel Nightingale.

All rights reserved.

No part of this book may be reproduced or transmitted in any form or by any means, electronic or mechanical, including photocopying, recording, or by any information storage and retrieval system, without permission in writing from the author.

This book was created with the assistance of an artificial intelligence program, and the author acknowledges the contributions of the program in the creation of this work.

This book is for entertainment purposes only. The information and advice contained within should not be used as a substitute for professional advice or guidance. The author and publisher are not responsible for any actions taken by the reader as a result of the information provided in this book. It is always recommended to consult with a professional in the field before making any significant changes in your life.

The Wardrobe that Drove Me Crazy 6

The Liberation of Minimalism 8

A Closet Full of Clothes and Nothing to Wear 10

The High Cost of Fast Fashion 12

The Joy of Decluttering 14

The Psychology of Clothing 16

The Beauty of Simplicity 18

The Philosophy of Minimalism 20

A New Beginning 22

The Capsule Wardrobe 24

Building a Minimalist Wardrobe 26

Curating Your Closet 30

Quality over Quantity 32

The Versatile Clothing Collection 34

Understanding Your Personal Style 36

Dressing with Purpose 38

Finding the Perfect Fit 40

The Importance of Texture and Fabric 42

Essential Pieces for Every Minimalist Wardrobe 44

The Power of Accessorizing 46

Minimalism for Every Season 48

Sustainable Fashion 51

The Art of Layering 54

The Minimalist Approach to Shoes 56

The Future of Minimalism and Clothing 58

Conclusion 60

The Wardrobe that Drove Me Crazy

It all started with a simple task: cleaning out my closet. But as I began to dig through the piles of clothes, I realized something was very wrong. I had way too much stuff. My closet was overflowing with clothes, shoes, and accessories, but I still felt like I had nothing to wear. Every morning, I would stand in front of my closet, paralyzed by the overwhelming amount of options. I was drowning in a sea of fabric and it was driving me crazy.

I had always loved fashion and I enjoyed experimenting with new styles and trends. But over time, my love of fashion had turned into an obsession with buying new clothes. I would scour the racks at the mall, searching for the latest styles and trends, and I couldn't resist making a purchase (or ten). I thought I was building a wardrobe, but what I was really doing was hoarding clothes.

As I continued to sort through my closet, I began to realize just how much money I had wasted on clothes that I had only worn once or twice. I had shirts with tags still on them and dresses that I had never even taken out of the plastic. I had shoes that were so uncomfortable, I could barely walk in them, and jewelry that I never wore. My closet was a mess, and my bank account was suffering because of it.

But it wasn't just the financial cost that was bothering me. It was the mental and emotional toll that my cluttered closet was taking on me. I felt stressed and overwhelmed every time I opened my closet doors. I was constantly worried about what I was going to wear, and I was spending far too much time and energy on something that should have been simple.

As I continued to clean out my closet, I began to research minimalist fashion and the idea of living with less. I read blogs and books on the subject, and I started to realize that there was a different way to approach my wardrobe. I didn't have to keep buying new clothes to feel good about myself, and I didn't have to keep up with every trend that came along. I could simplify my wardrobe and still feel stylish and put together.

It wasn't an easy process, but over time, I began to let go of the clothes that no longer served me. I donated bags of clothing to charity, sold some items online, and gave away others to friends and family. I started to focus on quality over quantity, and I invested in pieces that would last me for years, rather than just one season. I began to curate a wardrobe that was versatile, timeless, and reflective of my personal style.

And you know what? It was the best decision I ever made. I now have a wardrobe that I love and that makes me feel good about myself. Getting dressed in the morning is no longer a stressful experience, and I no longer feel the need to buy new clothes all the time. I'm not saying that everyone needs to become a minimalist, but for me, simplifying my wardrobe was a game-changer. It allowed me to focus on what's truly important in life, and it gave me a sense of peace and clarity that I never had before.

The Liberation of Minimalism

As I continued down the path of minimalism, I found that my relationship with my wardrobe was just the beginning. It was a gateway to a much larger journey of self-discovery and self-improvement. The liberation that came with minimizing my possessions was something that extended to every aspect of my life.

By simplifying my wardrobe, I had more time and energy to focus on the things that truly mattered to me. I started to prioritize experiences over possessions, and I found that I was able to enjoy life more fully. Instead of spending my weekends shopping or cleaning out my closet, I was able to spend time with my friends and family, pursuing my hobbies, and exploring the world around me.

I also found that minimalism helped me to clarify my priorities and values. As I started to let go of the things that no longer served me, I began to realize what was truly important to me. I started to focus on the relationships and activities that brought me joy and fulfillment, and I began to let go of the things that didn't.

One of the biggest areas of my life that was impacted by minimalism was my finances. By cutting out unnecessary expenses and focusing on what was truly important to me, I was able to save more money and live more intentionally. I started to make more thoughtful choices about how I spent my money, and I found that I was able to achieve financial goals that I had previously thought were impossible.

But perhaps the most profound impact of minimalism was on my mental and emotional health. By simplifying my life and minimizing the distractions and clutter around me, I found that I was able to focus more fully on the present moment. I was able to be more mindful, more grateful, and more content with my life as it was.

Of course, minimalism isn't a magic solution to all of life's problems. There are still challenges and struggles that come with the journey. But for me, the liberation that came with minimizing my possessions and simplifying my life was truly life-changing. It allowed me to live more fully and intentionally, and it gave me a sense of peace and contentment that I had never experienced before.

In the end, minimalism isn't about deprivation or restriction. It's about freedom and choice. It's about focusing on what truly matters and letting go of the rest. It's about living a life that is true to who you are and what you value. And for me, the liberation of minimalism was the key to unlocking a more joyful, fulfilling, and meaningful life.

A Closet Full of Clothes and Nothing to Wear

Have you ever stood in front of your closet, staring at a sea of clothes, feeling like you have nothing to wear? I know I have. It's a frustrating and all-too-common feeling, and it's something that I struggled with for years before I discovered the power of minimalism.

As a young adult, I fell into the trap that so many of us do: I believed that having more clothes would make me happy. I spent countless hours shopping, scouring sales racks and clearance bins for the latest trends and styles. I would come home with bags full of clothes, feeling excited and satisfied with my purchases.

But that feeling never lasted long. Soon enough, the excitement would fade, and I would be left with a closet full of clothes that I didn't really love or wear. I found myself constantly feeling like I had nothing to wear, even though my closet was overflowing.

It wasn't until I discovered minimalism that I began to understand the root of the problem. I realized that I had been equating my self-worth with the number of clothes I owned, rather than with who I was as a person. I had been buying into the idea that having more things would make me happier, when in reality it was just causing me stress and anxiety.

So, I decided to make a change. I began by decluttering my wardrobe, getting rid of the clothes that I didn't wear or didn't love. It was a difficult process at first, as I had to confront my attachment to certain items and the guilt I felt for spending money on things that I never wore. But as I let go of more and more, I found that I was left with a wardrobe that truly reflected my style and my personality.

As I continued to live with a minimalist wardrobe, I began to develop a more intentional approach to shopping. I stopped buying clothes just because they were on sale or because they were trendy, and instead focused on buying things that I truly loved and that fit with my existing wardrobe. I started to prioritize quality over quantity, investing in pieces that I knew would last for years rather than cheap items that would fall apart after a few wears.

And as I developed this intentional approach to my wardrobe, I found that the feeling of having nothing to wear became a thing of the past. I had fewer clothes, but each piece was carefully selected and well-loved. I no longer felt overwhelmed by choice, and instead felt confident and comfortable in what I was wearing.

Of course, the journey to a minimalist wardrobe isn't an easy one. It takes time, effort, and a willingness to let go of the attachment we have to our possessions. But for me, it was a journey that was well worth it. By decluttering my wardrobe and living with less, I was able to cultivate a sense of peace and contentment that I had never experienced before. And in the end, I realized that having a closet full of clothes doesn't necessarily lead to happiness – but having a wardrobe that reflects who you are can be a powerful step towards it.

The High Cost of Fast Fashion

There's no denying that the fashion industry is a massive force in our world, shaping the way we dress, the trends we follow, and even the way we see ourselves. But what many of us don't realize is the true cost of fast fashion: the toll it takes on our planet, our communities, and even our own wallets.

As a young adult, I was no stranger to the allure of fast fashion. I loved the thrill of finding a bargain, of snapping up the latest trends at rock-bottom prices. But it wasn't until I began to learn about the impact of fast fashion on our world that I realized the true cost of those seemingly cheap clothes.

One of the biggest problems with fast fashion is its impact on the environment. From the vast amounts of water used in the production of cotton, to the toxic chemicals released in the dyeing and finishing process, to the enormous amounts of waste created by the constant turnover of clothes, the fashion industry is one of the most polluting industries in the world.

But it's not just the planet that pays the price for fast fashion – it's also the people involved in its production. Many of the clothes we buy are made in developing countries, where workers are paid extremely low wages and often forced to work in unsafe and inhumane conditions. In many cases, these workers are children, who are denied the opportunity to go to school and build a better future for themselves and their families.

And even for those of us who don't directly feel the impact of fast fashion on our own lives, the true cost can be felt in our wallets. We've become so accustomed to cheap clothes that we've lost sight of the true value of quality, well-made garments. By constantly buying new clothes that fall apart after just a few wears, we're throwing our money away and contributing to a cycle of waste and environmental destruction.

But the good news is that there are alternatives. By embracing minimalism and focusing on quality over quantity, we can break free from the cycle of fast fashion and begin to make a real difference in the world. We can choose to support ethical and sustainable brands, or even better, we can choose to buy secondhand clothes and give them a new life.

For me, learning about the true cost of fast fashion was a wake-up call. It made me realize that the choices we make when we shop can have a real impact on the world around us. And it inspired me to change my own habits, to seek out brands and products that align with my values, and to support a more sustainable and ethical fashion industry.

In the end, it's up to each of us to decide what kind of impact we want to make with our fashion choices. But by understanding the true cost of fast fashion and taking action to make a difference, we can help create a better, more sustainable world for ourselves and future generations.

The Joy of Decluttering

As someone who once owned more clothes than she knew what to do with, I know all too well the weight of clutter. It's not just the physical clutter of a jam-packed closet or overflowing drawers, but the mental clutter of feeling overwhelmed and bogged down by our possessions. But when we begin to declutter, to let go of the things that no longer serve us, we can experience a sense of liberation and joy like no other.

For me, the journey toward minimalism began with a simple question: why do I own so much stuff? I began to take a closer look at my possessions, and I realized that many of them no longer brought me joy or served a useful purpose in my life. In fact, they were often a source of stress and anxiety, reminding me of the clutter and chaos that surrounded me.

So I began to declutter. I started with my clothes, sorting through each item and asking myself whether it was something I truly loved and wore regularly. If not, it went into a donation pile. As I let go of each piece, I felt a sense of relief and lightness, as though I was shedding a layer of the past that no longer served me.

The same process repeated with other areas of my life: books I'd read and would never pick up again, trinkets and souvenirs that had lost their meaning, and even digital clutter like old emails and files. With each item that left my life, I felt a growing sense of freedom and clarity.

But decluttering isn't just about getting rid of things – it's also about rediscovering the things that truly matter to us. When we let go of the excess, we're left with the things that we truly love and cherish. We can create space in our lives for the people and experiences that truly bring us joy.

For me, decluttering also had a ripple effect on other areas of my life. As I let go of physical clutter, I began to let go of mental clutter as well, shedding old habits and thought patterns that no longer served me. I became more mindful of the choices I was making, both in my possessions and in my daily life, and more intentional about creating a life that aligned with my values and goals.

The joy of decluttering isn't just about the act of letting go – it's about what comes next. It's about creating a life that's lighter, simpler, and more aligned with our true selves. It's about rediscovering the joy of what truly matters, and making space for the things that bring us true happiness and fulfillment.

In the end, the journey toward minimalism and decluttering isn't always easy. It can be a challenge to let go of the things we've held onto for so long, and to confront the deeper reasons behind our clutter. But when we do, we open ourselves up to a world of possibility, a world where joy, clarity, and freedom are waiting for us.

The Psychology of Clothing

It's no secret that the clothes we wear can have a powerful impact on our emotions and our behavior. From the way we feel when we put on our favorite outfit, to the way we present ourselves to the world, clothing can be a powerful tool for self-expression and communication. But what is it about clothing that has such a profound impact on our psychology?

One theory is that the clothes we wear can influence our state of mind through a process called enclothed cognition. Essentially, this means that the clothes we wear can trigger specific mental associations and emotions. For example, when we put on a suit or a professional outfit, we might feel more confident and capable, because those clothes are associated with competence and authority.

But the psychology of clothing goes much deeper than simple associations. Our clothing choices can be a reflection of our identity, our culture, and our values. They can signal to others who we are and what we believe in. They can also impact the way we're perceived by others, and the way we interact with the world around us.

For me, the psychology of clothing became especially apparent as I began to embrace minimalism and intentional living. I realized that the clothes I wore were a reflection of my values and my personality, and that I could use my clothing choices to express myself in a more authentic way.

I began to pay more attention to the quality of the clothes I wore, choosing pieces that were well-made and sustainable, rather than disposable fast fashion. I also became more intentional about the colors and styles that I chose, selecting items that made me feel confident and comfortable, rather than just following trends or societal expectations.

As I made these changes, I noticed a profound shift in the way I felt about myself and the world around me. I felt more connected to my values and my identity, and more confident in my ability to express myself authentically. I also noticed that I was more aware of the impact of my clothing choices on the world, and more committed to making choices that aligned with my beliefs and my goals.

But the psychology of clothing isn't just about our individual choices – it's also about the larger social and cultural context in which we live. Our clothing choices can be influenced by a wide range of factors, from our economic status to our cultural background, and they can signal to others a wide range of meanings and messages. For example, in some cultures, specific colors or styles of clothing may be associated with particular social or religious groups, and wearing those clothes can be a way of signaling one's membership in that group. In other contexts, clothing choices may be influenced by societal expectations or pressure to conform to certain standards of beauty or style.

Ultimately, the psychology of clothing is a complex and multifaceted topic, one that touches on everything from our personal identity to our social and cultural context. By paying attention to the way our clothing choices impact our emotions and behavior, we can become more mindful of the role clothing plays in our lives, and more intentional about the messages we're sending to the world.

The Beauty of Simplicity

In a world that often seems obsessed with excess, with accumulating more and more possessions, there is a growing movement of people who are embracing simplicity. This movement is about more than just decluttering and minimizing – it's about recognizing the beauty and value of a simpler, more intentional way of life.

At its heart, simplicity is about finding joy and fulfillment in the things that truly matter – family, friends, experiences, and the natural world around us. It's about recognizing that we don't need a constant stream of new possessions to be happy or fulfilled, and that sometimes less is truly more.

For me, the beauty of simplicity became apparent as I began to embrace minimalism and intentional living. I discovered that by letting go of excess possessions and focusing on the things that truly mattered, I felt more connected to the world around me and more at peace with myself.

I began to appreciate the beauty in simplicity – in the unadorned natural world, in the simple pleasures of time spent with loved ones, and in the pared-down aesthetic of a well-curated wardrobe. I found that by stripping away the excess, I was able to see more clearly the beauty that existed in the world around me.

Of course, embracing simplicity isn't always easy. It can mean letting go of deeply ingrained cultural and societal expectations, and it can require a willingness to be vulnerable and open to new experiences. It can also mean confronting difficult emotions and coming to terms with the things that truly matter in our lives.

But the rewards of simplicity are many. By focusing on the things that truly matter, we can build deeper connections with those around us, and find more meaning and purpose in our lives. We can also reduce our impact on the environment and live more sustainably, creating a better world for future generations.

In the end, the beauty of simplicity is about more than just decluttering our physical possessions. It's about recognizing the value and beauty in the simple things in life, and finding joy in the present moment. By embracing simplicity, we can create a more intentional and fulfilling way of life, one that celebrates the things that truly matter and brings us closer to the people and world around us.

The Philosophy of Minimalism

Minimalism is more than just a way of decluttering our homes or simplifying our wardrobes. It's a philosophy that can have a profound impact on the way we live our lives and the way we interact with the world around us.

At its core, the philosophy of minimalism is about living with intention and purpose. It's about recognizing the things that truly matter in our lives and letting go of the things that don't. It's about living in a way that is mindful, deliberate, and conscious of the impact we have on the world.

For me, the philosophy of minimalism has been a journey of self-discovery and personal growth. It has required me to question my own values and beliefs, and to reevaluate the way I live my life.

Through minimalism, I have come to recognize the value of living with less, of letting go of excess possessions and focusing on the things that truly matter. I have discovered the importance of living sustainably, of being mindful of my impact on the environment, and of living in a way that is both conscious and intentional.

At the heart of the philosophy of minimalism is the recognition that happiness and fulfillment cannot be found in material possessions. Instead, true happiness comes from living a life that is aligned with our values, and that brings us joy and meaning.

Minimalism also requires us to be mindful of the impact we have on the world. By consuming less and living more sustainably, we can reduce our impact on the environment and create a better world for future generations.

But perhaps most importantly, the philosophy of minimalism is about creating space in our lives – space for meaningful connections with loved ones, space for personal growth and development, and space for the things that truly matter.

By embracing the philosophy of minimalism, we can create a life that is more intentional, more fulfilling, and more meaningful. We can live in a way that is conscious of our impact on the world, and that recognizes the value of the things that truly matter.

A New Beginning

As I sat in my newly decluttered and minimalist home, I couldn't help but feel a sense of calm and contentment wash over me. My life had been transformed by the philosophy of minimalism, and I was eager to continue on this journey towards a simpler and more intentional life.

But as with any journey, there were bound to be bumps in the road. Even with the best of intentions, it's easy to slip back into old habits and ways of thinking.

That's why it's important to view minimalism as a journey, rather than a destination. It's a continuous process of growth and self-discovery, and there will always be new challenges and opportunities for growth.

For me, the biggest challenge was learning to let go of my attachment to material possessions. As someone who had always found comfort in things, it was difficult to learn to live with less.

But with time, I began to realize that the true source of happiness and fulfillment was not in material possessions, but in the relationships and experiences that I had in my life. By focusing on what truly mattered to me, I was able to let go of the things that didn't, and create space for the things that did.

I also began to appreciate the beauty of simplicity in all aspects of my life. From my wardrobe to my home, I began to embrace a more minimal and streamlined approach, and found that it brought me a sense of peace and clarity.

And as I continued on this journey, I discovered new opportunities for growth and learning. I found that minimalism had opened up new avenues for personal development, and that I was becoming a more mindful and intentional person in all aspects of my life.

But perhaps most importantly, I found that minimalism had given me a sense of purpose and meaning in my life. By living intentionally and consciously, I felt that I was making a positive impact on the world, and that my actions were aligned with my values and beliefs.

As I reflect back on my journey, I can't help but feel grateful for the lessons that minimalism has taught me. It has transformed my life in so many ways, and I know that this journey is far from over.

But with each new challenge, I feel more equipped to handle it, and more confident in my ability to live a life that is simple, intentional, and fulfilling. A new beginning has truly emerged, and I am excited to see where this journey will take me next.

The Capsule Wardrobe

As I delved deeper into the world of minimalism and intentional living, I came across the concept of the capsule wardrobe. At first, I was skeptical - how could a wardrobe with only a handful of items be practical or stylish?

But as I began to explore the idea further, I realized that a capsule wardrobe wasn't about limiting yourself - it was about curating a collection of clothes that truly reflected your personal style, while also being versatile and functional.

The key to a successful capsule wardrobe, I learned, was choosing a color palette and sticking to it. By selecting a few neutral colors that complemented each other, I could easily mix and match my clothes, creating a variety of outfits with just a few key pieces.

I also discovered that a capsule wardrobe was not meant to be static - it was a living, breathing entity that could be adapted and modified to suit your needs and lifestyle. As the seasons changed or my personal style evolved, I could add or remove items from my wardrobe, always keeping it fresh and up-to-date.

One of the biggest benefits of a capsule wardrobe, I found, was the sense of ease and simplicity it brought to my daily life. No longer did I spend hours agonizing over what to wear - I could simply reach for a few key pieces and be confident in my outfit choice.

And as I began to build my own capsule wardrobe, I found that it wasn't as difficult as I had originally thought. I started by selecting a few key pieces - a versatile pair of pants, a classic blazer, and a comfortable pair of shoes - and built my collection from there.

As I added new pieces, I made sure they were functional, versatile, and aligned with my personal style. I also made a conscious effort to shop ethically and sustainably, choosing items that were made to last and had a minimal impact on the environment.

Today, my capsule wardrobe is a reflection of who I am and what I value. It's a collection of clothes that are both practical and stylish, and that make me feel confident and comfortable in my own skin.

And while the idea of a capsule wardrobe may seem daunting at first, I encourage anyone who is interested to give it a try. You may be surprised at how liberating and empowering it can be to simplify your wardrobe and focus on what truly matters.

Building a Minimalist Wardrobe

As I embarked on my journey towards minimalism, one of the biggest challenges I faced was redefining my relationship with clothes. For so long, I had equated material possessions with success and happiness, and my closet was a physical manifestation of that mindset - overflowing with clothes, shoes, and accessories that I rarely wore or appreciated.

But as I began to embrace minimalism, I realized that building a wardrobe of high-quality, functional, and timeless pieces was not only possible, but also incredibly empowering. By focusing on quality over quantity, I could create a wardrobe that truly reflected my personal style and values, while also being practical and versatile.

So, how does one go about building a minimalist wardrobe? It's a process that takes time and intentionality, but the end result is well worth the effort. Here are some steps that helped me along the way:

1. Identify your personal style

Before you start shopping for new clothes, it's important to have a clear idea of what you want your wardrobe to look like. Spend some time browsing fashion blogs or Instagram accounts to get inspiration, and make a list of the styles, colors, and fabrics that appeal to you.

2. Assess your current wardrobe

Once you have a clear idea of your personal style, it's time to take a hard look at your current wardrobe. Which items do you wear frequently, and which ones are gathering dust in the back of your closet? Consider donating or selling any items that no longer serve you, and focus on building a wardrobe of high-quality, functional pieces that you will wear and appreciate for years to come.

3. Invest in quality basics

Every wardrobe needs a foundation of high-quality basics that can be mixed and matched with other items. Think classic pieces like a white t-shirt, a pair of black pants, or a denim jacket - these items never go out of style and can be dressed up or down depending on the occasion.

4. Shop mindfully

As you start to build your minimalist wardrobe, make a conscious effort to shop mindfully. Consider buying secondhand or from sustainable and ethical brands, and prioritize quality over price. When you do buy new clothes, make sure they align with your personal style and values, and that they will be a valuable addition to your wardrobe.

5. Keep it simple

Finally, remember that minimalism is about simplifying your life, not complicating it. Don't get bogged down in the details - focus on building a wardrobe that you love and that works for your lifestyle, and don't be afraid to experiment and try new things.

As I began to build my own minimalist wardrobe, I found that the process was both challenging and rewarding. It forced me to reassess my values and priorities, and to let go of the idea that material possessions equate to happiness.

Today, my wardrobe is a reflection of who I am and what I stand for - a collection of clothes that are both functional and stylish, and that make me feel confident and comfortable in my own skin. And while the journey towards building a minimalist wardrobe may be long and winding, the end result is well worth the effort.

Curating Your Closet

The process of curating a minimalist wardrobe can be a challenging one, requiring a great deal of thought, care, and attention to detail. However, it is also a deeply rewarding process that can help you to streamline your life and focus on the things that truly matter.

To begin with, it is important to take a good, hard look at the clothes you currently own. As we discussed earlier in this book, many of us tend to accumulate far more clothes than we actually need, often without even realizing it. Therefore, it is important to take some time to go through your closet and assess what you really use and love, and what is just taking up space.

When curating your closet, it is important to think in terms of quality over quantity. Instead of buying lots of cheap, trendy clothes that will fall apart after a few wears, focus on investing in high-quality, timeless pieces that will last for years to come. These might include a well-made pair of jeans, a classic trench coat, or a simple, elegant dress.

Another important consideration when curating your wardrobe is to think about your personal style. What kind of clothes do you feel most comfortable and confident in? What colors and patterns do you tend to gravitate towards? By understanding your own unique style, you can make more informed choices about what to keep and what to let go of in your closet.

Finally, it is important to remember that building a minimalist wardrobe is not something that can be accomplished overnight. It is a gradual process, one that requires patience and persistence. But if you are willing to put in the time and effort, you can create a wardrobe that truly reflects your values and your personality, and that brings you joy and satisfaction every time you get dressed.

For me, the process of curating my own minimalist wardrobe was a deeply transformative experience. I realized that I had been holding onto clothes that no longer served me, simply because I felt guilty about getting rid of them. But once I let go of that guilt and began to focus on what truly mattered to me, I was able to create a closet that felt like a true reflection of who I am.

One of my favorite pieces in my minimalist wardrobe is a simple, tailored blazer that I bought several years ago. It is made from high-quality wool, and it fits me perfectly. I wear it with everything from jeans and a t-shirt to a fancy dress, and it always makes me feel confident and put-together.

Overall, I believe that curating a minimalist wardrobe is a wonderful way to simplify your life, reduce your environmental impact, and express your unique sense of style. With a little patience, persistence, and care, anyone can create a wardrobe that brings them joy and satisfaction every day.

Quality over Quantity

When it comes to building a minimalist wardrobe, one of the most important principles to keep in mind is quality over quantity. This means investing in high-quality pieces that are built to last, rather than buying cheap, trendy clothes that will quickly fall apart.

There are a number of reasons why prioritizing quality over quantity is so important. For one thing, high-quality clothes are often made from superior materials and with better construction techniques, which means they are more durable and less likely to wear out or become damaged. This, in turn, can save you money in the long run, as you won't have to constantly replace your clothes.

In addition to being more durable, high-quality clothes are often more comfortable and more flattering than their cheaper counterparts. This is because they are designed with more attention to detail, and are often made with a greater emphasis on fit and comfort. For example, a well-made pair of jeans will fit you like a glove, whereas a cheap pair might sag in all the wrong places and feel uncomfortable to wear.

Another important benefit of prioritizing quality over quantity is that it can help to reduce your environmental impact. When we buy cheap, disposable clothes, we are contributing to the culture of fast fashion, which has a devastating effect on the planet. By investing in high-quality clothes that are built to last, we can reduce the amount of clothing that ends up in landfills and do our part to protect the environment.

For me, the value of quality over quantity really hit home when I invested in a high-quality leather jacket several years ago. At the time, it felt like a big splurge, but I knew that it was something I would wear for years to come. And I was right - I have worn that jacket countless times, and it still looks just as beautiful and timeless as it did the day I bought it. Every time I put it on, I feel a sense of joy and satisfaction knowing that I made a smart investment in a piece that will last a lifetime.

Overall, I believe that prioritizing quality over quantity is an essential part of building a minimalist wardrobe that truly reflects your values and your sense of style. By investing in high-quality pieces that are built to last, we can reduce our environmental impact, save money in the long run, and feel great about what we wear every day.

The Versatile Clothing Collection

One of the key principles of a minimalist wardrobe is versatility, and this is where the concept of a versatile clothing collection comes into play. A versatile collection consists of a carefully curated selection of clothes that can be mixed and matched in a variety of different ways, allowing you to create a wide range of outfits with just a few key pieces.

The benefits of a versatile collection are numerous. For one thing, it can help you to get more use out of the clothes you already own, as you'll be able to wear them in different combinations and contexts. This can help to reduce the amount of clothing you need to buy, which in turn can save you money and reduce your environmental impact.

Another benefit of a versatile collection is that it can make getting dressed in the morning much easier and more enjoyable. Rather than staring at a closet full of clothes and feeling overwhelmed, you'll be able to quickly and easily put together outfits that you know will look great and make you feel confident.

So what does a versatile clothing collection look like in practice? The key is to focus on pieces that can be dressed up or down, and that can be worn in a variety of different ways. This might include classic items like a well-fitting pair of jeans, a tailored blazer, and a simple black dress, as well as more trend-driven pieces that can be layered and mixed and matched.

For example, I have a versatile collection that includes a few key pieces that I can wear in a variety of different ways. One of my go-to items is a pair of black ankle boots that I can wear with everything from jeans to dresses to skirts. I also have a classic trench coat that I can dress up or down, depending on the occasion.

In addition to these staples, I like to incorporate a few more trend-driven pieces into my versatile collection each season. For example, this year I invested in a lightweight midi skirt in a fun print, which I can wear with a simple t-shirt and sandals for a casual look, or dress up with a blouse and heels for a more formal occasion.

Ultimately, the key to building a versatile clothing collection is to focus on quality, timeless pieces that can be mixed and matched in a variety of different ways. By doing so, you'll be able to create a wardrobe that truly reflects your sense of style and that makes getting dressed in the morning a breeze.

Understanding Your Personal Style

As we have seen, minimalism is all about simplifying your life, and one of the best ways to do this is to understand your personal style. It's about knowing what you like and what makes you feel comfortable and confident. In this chapter, we'll explore the concept of personal style and how it can be applied to building a minimalist wardrobe.

When it comes to understanding your personal style, there are a few things you need to consider. The first is your lifestyle. Are you a busy mom who is always on the go, or do you work in an office and need to dress professionally? Your lifestyle will have a big impact on the types of clothes you need and the style that will work best for you.

The second thing to consider is your body type. Are you tall or short? Do you have a curvy figure or a more athletic build? Understanding your body type will help you find clothes that flatter your figure and make you feel great.

Once you have a good idea of your lifestyle and body type, it's time to start exploring your personal style. Do you like classic, timeless pieces, or are you more drawn to trendy, edgy looks? Do you prefer bold colors and patterns, or do you like to keep things simple with neutral tones? These are all questions that can help you define your personal style.

One of the best ways to explore your personal style is to create a mood board. This can be done using Pinterest, magazine clippings, or any other visual medium that speaks to you. Collect images of outfits, accessories, and styles that you love and that make you feel inspired. Over time, you will start to see patterns emerging in the images you collect, and this will help you define your personal style even further.

When it comes to building a minimalist wardrobe, understanding your personal style is key. This will help you choose pieces that you love and that you will wear over and over again. It's all about quality over quantity, and investing in pieces that you know you will wear and that will last for years to come.

For me personally, I've always been drawn to classic, timeless pieces. I love neutral colors like black, white, and beige, and I tend to shy away from bold patterns and bright colors. When I started my minimalist journey, I knew that I wanted to focus on building a wardrobe full of pieces that I loved and that I knew I would wear for years to come. I invested in a few high-quality, classic pieces like a black blazer, a white button-down shirt, and a pair of high-quality jeans, and these have become the foundation of my wardrobe.

Understanding your personal style is a journey, and it's one that will evolve over time. The key is to stay true to yourself and to invest in pieces that make you feel confident and comfortable. With a little time and effort, you can build a minimalist wardrobe that reflects your personal style and simplifies your life.

Dressing with Purpose

As I mentioned in a previous chapter, clothing is not just about appearance. It can have a significant impact on our mindset and even our daily activities. When we dress with purpose, we are making a conscious effort to use our clothing to achieve specific goals, whether that be feeling more confident, professional, or relaxed. In this chapter, we will explore the concept of dressing with purpose and how it can benefit us in our daily lives.

Dressing with purpose begins with identifying your goals for the day or the event you are attending. What do you want to accomplish, and how do you want to feel? Once you have a clear understanding of what you want to achieve, you can choose clothing that supports those goals. For example, if you are attending a job interview, you might choose a suit or a dress that makes you feel confident and professional. On the other hand, if you are going for a walk in the park, you might choose clothing that is comfortable and easy to move in.

It's important to note that dressing with purpose doesn't necessarily mean dressing up. It's about choosing clothing that helps you achieve your goals, whatever they may be. For some people, that might mean wearing a suit every day, while for others, it might mean wearing comfortable clothing that allows them to move freely.

Dressing with purpose can also help you avoid decision fatigue. When we have too many choices, it can be overwhelming, and we can become indecisive. By limiting our clothing choices to a curated selection that serves a specific purpose, we can simplify our lives and make it easier to get ready in the morning.

Another benefit of dressing with purpose is that it can help us stay focused and motivated. When we dress for success, we are more likely to feel confident and capable of achieving our goals. This can translate into increased productivity and a more positive outlook on life.

Personal Example:

I remember a time when I was feeling particularly unmotivated and lacked direction in my life. I was working from home, and every day felt like a struggle to get anything done. I decided to try dressing with purpose, even though I was only going to be working from home. I chose clothing that was comfortable yet professional and made me feel confident. To my surprise, I found that I was more productive and had a better attitude towards work. Dressing with purpose helped me focus on my goals and gave me the motivation I needed to move forward.

In conclusion, dressing with purpose can be a powerful tool in achieving our goals and living a more fulfilling life. By identifying our goals and choosing clothing that supports them, we can simplify our lives, stay focused and motivated, and feel confident in our abilities to achieve success.

Finding the Perfect Fit

The process of finding the perfect fit when it comes to clothing is essential in creating a minimalist wardrobe. One of the reasons why we end up with too many clothes is because we buy items that don't fit us properly, so we don't wear them, and they end up at the back of our closet.

Finding the perfect fit takes time and patience, but it's worth the effort. Once you know your body type and what styles suit you, you'll be able to make more informed decisions when it comes to purchasing new clothing.

The first step is to understand your body type. Knowing whether you are an apple, pear, hourglass, or rectangle shape will help you choose clothes that will flatter your figure. For example, if you have an apple-shaped body, you might want to focus on clothes that cinch at the waist to create a more defined silhouette.

It's also essential to understand your measurements. Knowing your measurements will help you determine your size accurately and will prevent you from buying clothes that are too big or too small. You can measure yourself at home using a tape measure or go to a tailor or a clothing store and have them measure you.

Once you have an idea of your body type and measurements, it's time to try on clothes. When you're in the store, take the time to try on different styles and sizes. Don't be afraid to ask the sales associate for help or advice, as they can be a valuable resource.

When you're trying on clothes, pay attention to how they fit in different areas. For example, when trying on pants, check how they fit around the waist, hips, and thighs. Are they too tight or too loose? Do they bunch up at the bottom? Are they too long or too short? By asking yourself these questions, you'll be able to determine whether or not the item is a good fit for you.

Another important factor to consider when finding the perfect fit is the fabric of the clothing. Different fabrics can affect how a piece of clothing fits and feels. For example, a stretchy fabric might be more forgiving in terms of fit, while a stiffer fabric might require a more exact fit.

Finding the perfect fit can take time and effort, but it's worth it in the end. When you have clothes that fit you well and make you feel confident, you'll be more likely to wear them and less likely to buy new items unnecessarily.

Personally, finding the perfect fit has been a game-changer for me. I used to struggle with finding clothes that fit me properly, and I often ended up with items that were either too tight or too loose. Once I took the time to understand my body type and measurements, I was able to make more informed decisions when it came to purchasing new clothes. Now, I have a wardrobe full of items that fit me well, and I feel confident in what I'm wearing every day.

The Importance of Texture and Fabric

Texture and fabric play a crucial role in the way we experience clothing. They can make a garment feel luxurious, comfortable, and elegant or cheap, scratchy, and uncomfortable. Choosing the right fabric and texture can elevate a simple outfit and make it stand out. In this chapter, we'll explore the importance of texture and fabric in building a minimalist wardrobe.

When it comes to texture, we often focus on the way a garment feels to the touch. Soft cashmere, smooth silk, and cozy wool are all textures that we tend to seek out. But texture is also about the visual aspect of a garment. For example, a piece with a unique texture, such as a chunky knit sweater, can add dimension and interest to an outfit. It's essential to consider both the tactile and visual texture of a garment when choosing pieces for a minimalist wardrobe.

When it comes to fabric, there are several factors to consider. Quality is one of the most crucial elements. High-quality fabrics, such as silk, wool, and cotton, not only feel better on the skin but also last longer. Investing in quality fabrics can save you money in the long run by reducing the need to replace clothing frequently.

Another important consideration when choosing fabrics is their environmental impact. Many fabrics, such as polyester and nylon, are made from synthetic materials that are harmful to the environment. Choosing natural materials, such as organic cotton or linen, can reduce your environmental footprint.

One of the most significant advantages of a minimalist wardrobe is that it allows us to invest in high-quality fabrics that we love. When we have fewer pieces of clothing, we can afford to spend more on each piece. This means we can buy pieces that are made from luxurious fabrics, which we may not have been able to afford before.

In my experience, investing in quality fabrics has made a significant difference in the way I feel in my clothing. I used to buy cheap clothing made from synthetic materials because it was all I could afford. But as I started to embrace minimalism, I began to invest in high-quality fabrics. I purchased a silk blouse that felt like butter against my skin and a wool coat that kept me warm on even the coldest days. I found that I enjoyed getting dressed more when I was wearing pieces that felt luxurious and well-made.

In conclusion, the textures and fabrics we choose are a crucial part of building a minimalist wardrobe. By investing in quality fabrics and choosing pieces with interesting textures, we can elevate our wardrobes and create outfits that are both comfortable and visually appealing. We can also reduce our environmental impact by choosing natural materials and investing in pieces that will last for years to come.

Essential Pieces for Every Minimalist Wardrobe

As a minimalist, it's important to focus on quality, versatility, and longevity when curating your wardrobe. Here are some essential pieces that should be in every minimalist's wardrobe:

1. White t-shirt: A classic white t-shirt is a versatile and timeless staple that can be dressed up or down. It's important to invest in a high-quality t-shirt that will last a long time.
2. Little black dress: A well-fitting little black dress is a must-have in any minimalist's wardrobe. It can be dressed up or down and is perfect for any occasion.
3. High-waisted jeans: A good pair of high-waisted jeans is a great investment as they are incredibly versatile and can be paired with anything.
4. Blazer: A blazer is a great piece to dress up any outfit. It can be worn over a dress or with a t-shirt and jeans for a more casual look.
5. Cashmere sweater: A cashmere sweater is a great investment piece as it will last a long time and keep you warm during the colder months.
6. Leather jacket: A leather jacket is a great investment as it can be worn with a variety of outfits and will last a long time with proper care.
7. Midi skirt: A midi skirt is a versatile piece that can be dressed up or down. It can be worn with a t-shirt and sneakers or dressed up with heels and a blouse.
8. White sneakers: White sneakers are a classic and versatile shoe that can be worn with any outfit.

9. Classic trench coat: A classic trench coat is a must-have in any minimalist's wardrobe. It's a timeless piece that can be worn year after year.
10. Black pumps: A classic pair of black pumps can be dressed up or down and are perfect for any occasion.

These ten pieces are just a starting point for building a minimalist wardrobe. It's important to focus on quality and versatility when selecting pieces for your wardrobe. With these essential pieces, you'll be able to create a variety of outfits with just a few key items.

The Power of Accessorizing

As fashion icons throughout history have shown, accessories can make or break an outfit. The right accessory can take an outfit from drab to fab, while the wrong accessory can be a fashion disaster. But beyond just making an outfit look good, accessories can also serve a functional purpose, such as keeping you warm or carrying your essentials.

As a minimalist, it's important to carefully curate your accessories to ensure they add value to your wardrobe without cluttering it up. In this chapter, we'll explore the power of accessorizing and how to do it effectively.

One of the most important things to consider when accessorizing is your personal style. Just like with clothing, your accessories should reflect your unique personality and taste. Are you someone who loves statement jewelry or do you prefer dainty pieces? Do you like bold colors or muted tones? These are all things to consider when selecting accessories.

Another thing to keep in mind is the occasion. While some accessories are versatile enough to be worn in any setting, others are better suited for specific events. For example, a statement necklace might be perfect for a night out, but not appropriate for a business meeting.

When it comes to accessorizing as a minimalist, it's important to focus on quality over quantity. Instead of having a collection of cheap, trendy accessories that will only last for a season, invest in a few high-quality pieces that will stand the test of time. This not only saves you money in the long run, but it also ensures that your accessories won't contribute to the fast fashion cycle. Here are a few essential accessories:

1. A versatile scarf: Scarves are not only stylish, but also functional. They can keep you warm in the winter and add a pop of color to an otherwise neutral outfit. Look for a scarf made of high-quality fabric, such as cashmere or silk.
2. Classic sunglasses: Sunglasses not only protect your eyes from the sun, but also add a touch of sophistication to any outfit. Look for a classic style that will never go out of fashion, such as aviators or wayfarers.
3. A statement watch: A watch is not only a functional accessory, but also a statement piece that can add a touch of elegance to any outfit. Look for a classic style with a simple face and a leather or metal band.
4. A versatile handbag: Instead of having a collection of handbags for every occasion, invest in one high-quality, versatile bag that can be dressed up or down. Look for a classic style in a neutral color, such as black or brown.
5. Simple jewelry: Instead of having a collection of trendy, costume jewelry, invest in a few simple, high-quality pieces that can be worn with anything. Look for classic styles, such as stud earrings or a simple necklace, that will never go out of fashion.

As a minimalist, it's important to remember that accessories should add value to your wardrobe, not clutter it up. By carefully curating your accessories and focusing on quality over quantity, you can create a collection that not only looks great, but also serves a functional purpose.

Minimalism for Every Season

As the seasons change, so do our wardrobes. However, minimalism doesn't have to be limited to a particular season. In fact, the principles of minimalism can be applied to any season. In this chapter, we'll explore how to incorporate minimalism into every season of the year.

Spring:

Spring is a time of rebirth and renewal, and the same can be said for your wardrobe. As the weather starts to warm up, it's time to shed those heavy winter layers and opt for lighter, brighter pieces. A minimalist approach to spring dressing means choosing pieces that can be mixed and matched easily, and that can be worn in a variety of ways.

Personal example: For me, this means investing in a few key pieces, like a versatile trench coat, a pair of high-waisted jeans, and a classic white T-shirt. These pieces can be worn together or separately, and they provide a great foundation for any spring outfit.

Summer:

Summer is all about light and airy clothing that keeps you cool in the heat. A minimalist approach to summer dressing means choosing pieces that are both functional and stylish. Opt for pieces that can be dressed up or down, and that can be worn in a variety of settings.

Personal example: For me, this means investing in a few key pieces, like a lightweight sundress, a pair of comfortable sandals, and a wide-brimmed hat. These pieces can be worn to the beach or to a backyard barbecue, and they can be dressed up with a statement necklace or dressed down with a pair of sunglasses.

Fall:

Fall is a time of transition, and the same can be said for your wardrobe. As the weather starts to cool down, it's time to start layering up. A minimalist approach to fall dressing means choosing pieces that can be layered easily and that can be worn in a variety of ways.

Personal example: For me, this means investing in a few key pieces, like a warm sweater, a pair of comfortable ankle boots, and a versatile scarf. These pieces can be worn together or separately, and they provide a great foundation for any fall outfit.

Winter:

Winter is a time of warmth and coziness, and the same can be said for your wardrobe. As the weather gets colder, it's time to start layering up and incorporating warm and cozy pieces into your wardrobe. A minimalist approach to winter dressing means choosing pieces that are both functional and stylish.

Personal example: For me, this means investing in a few key pieces, like a warm coat, a pair of insulated boots, and a cozy hat and gloves. These pieces can be worn together or separately, and they provide a great foundation for any winter outfit.

No matter what season it is, a minimalist approach to dressing can help you streamline your wardrobe and make getting dressed in the morning a breeze. By choosing versatile pieces that can be mixed and matched easily, you can create a wardrobe that is both functional and stylish.

Sustainable Fashion

The subject of sustainable fashion had been a growing concern for many years, but only recently had it been getting the attention it deserves. It was not long ago that fashion lovers and fashionistas alike turned a blind eye to the negative impact that fashion had on the environment. The fashion industry had a reputation for being wasteful, exploitative, and lacking in ethical standards. However, things were changing, and people were starting to realize that something needed to be done. In this chapter, we will explore the world of sustainable fashion, and how it has evolved over the years.

Sustainable fashion is not a new concept, but it has gained traction in recent years as the world has become more aware of the negative impact of consumerism on the planet. Sustainable fashion aims to reduce the environmental impact of clothing production, from the sourcing of materials to the manufacturing process and distribution. This is done by using eco-friendly and sustainable materials, reducing waste, and promoting ethical labor practices.

One of the biggest concerns with the fashion industry is the waste that it generates. Every year, millions of tons of textiles are thrown away, either because they are no longer fashionable or because they are damaged beyond repair. The good news is that there are solutions to this problem. Sustainable fashion designers are using recycled materials and waste reduction techniques to create clothing that has a positive impact on the environment.

One example of a sustainable material is organic cotton. Conventional cotton production uses large amounts of pesticides and water, which can be harmful to the environment and the people involved in its production. Organic cotton, on the other hand, is grown without the use of harmful chemicals and is a more sustainable alternative.

Another material gaining popularity in sustainable fashion is recycled polyester. Recycled polyester is made from recycled plastic bottles and other waste materials. This process reduces the amount of plastic waste in landfills and the ocean and decreases the amount of energy required to produce new polyester.

Sustainable fashion is not just about using eco-friendly materials; it is also about reducing waste. One way this is achieved is through the use of upcycling. Upcycling is the process of transforming old or discarded materials into new products. This process not only reduces waste but also creates unique and one-of-a-kind pieces.

As for ethical labor practices, sustainable fashion designers are making sure that their clothing is produced under fair and humane working conditions. This means that workers are paid fair wages, work reasonable hours, and are not subjected to any form of exploitation.

In recent years, sustainable fashion has gained popularity with consumers who are becoming more conscious of their impact on the environment. Many people are now choosing to buy from sustainable brands, and even major fashion retailers are starting to make changes to become more sustainable.

As a personal example, I had always been passionate about fashion but was not aware of the impact it had on the environment. When I learned about sustainable fashion, I started to research and look for brands that were eco-friendly and ethical. I was amazed to find that there were so many beautiful and stylish sustainable options available. Not only did I feel good about my purchases, but I also felt like I was contributing to a better world.

In conclusion, sustainable fashion is the future of the fashion industry. It is important that we all do our part in reducing our environmental impact, and sustainable fashion is a great place to start. By choosing eco-friendly and ethical options, we can create a better world for ourselves and future generations.

The Art of Layering

In the world of fashion, there is an art to layering that can make all the difference in a well-put-together outfit. The skilled minimalist knows how to use layering to create visual interest, add warmth and texture to a look, and to extend the versatility of a wardrobe.

It's all about choosing the right fabrics, textures, and colors to make the layers work together seamlessly. You don't want to end up looking like a walking pile of clothes! When done right, layering can make your outfit look more expensive, polished, and cohesive.

When it comes to layering, one key aspect to consider is proportion. Mixing and matching different lengths and silhouettes can create a dynamic look that is both balanced and stylish. For example, a long tunic over slim-fit pants, topped with a cropped jacket, can create a flattering and versatile look that works for any occasion.

Another aspect of layering to consider is color. Choosing a monochromatic or complementary color palette can create a sleek and sophisticated look, while mixing and matching contrasting colors can add a playful and bold touch. It's all about experimenting and finding the right balance that works for your personal style.

Personally, I've found that layering is a key component of my minimalist wardrobe. I have a few simple and versatile pieces that I can mix and match in different ways to create a variety of outfits. For example, I have a slim-fit black turtleneck that I can wear on its own, or layered under a sweater or blazer for added warmth and texture. I also have a few lightweight scarves that I can use to add color and interest to my outfits.

The key to successful layering is to start with a solid foundation of high-quality basics and build from there. Invest in versatile pieces that can be dressed up or down, and that work for different occasions and seasons. With the right combination of layers, you can create a stylish and functional wardrobe that works for you.

The Minimalist Approach to Shoes

As a minimalist, it's essential to make sure that every item in your closet serves a purpose and that includes your shoes. The right pair of shoes can make or break an outfit and add a touch of style and sophistication. In this chapter, we'll explore the minimalist approach to shoes and how you can curate a collection that fits your personal style and lifestyle.

First and foremost, when it comes to minimalist shoes, quality is key. Invest in shoes made of durable materials that can withstand the test of time. While a quality pair of shoes may be more expensive upfront, in the long run, it's a cost-effective solution as you won't need to replace them as frequently.

Another essential factor to consider when building a minimalist shoe collection is versatility. Choose shoes that can work for multiple occasions and that pair well with the rest of your wardrobe. Neutral tones such as black, white, tan, and grey are great options as they are easy to match and work well with many different colors.

It's also important to think about the types of shoes that are most practical for your lifestyle. For example, if you walk a lot, you might need a comfortable and supportive pair of sneakers. If you work in a more formal environment, a classic pair of leather loafers may be more suitable. Consider what types of shoes you wear most often and invest in high-quality options that will last for years.

When it comes to personal examples, I remember buying a pair of black ankle boots a few years ago that were made of high-quality leather. They were comfortable to wear and could easily transition from work to a night out. I still wear them to this day and get compliments on them regularly. Another example is a pair of white sneakers I recently purchased. They are made of a durable material and match with many different outfits, making them a versatile and practical addition to my minimalist shoe collection.

In summary, when building a minimalist shoe collection, remember to focus on quality, versatility, and practicality. Invest in shoes made of durable materials and that can work for multiple occasions. Choose neutral tones and styles that fit your personal style and lifestyle. By following these simple tips, you can build a shoe collection that is both functional and fashionable.

The Future of Minimalism and Clothing

As we look to the future, it is important to consider the impact of our choices on the world around us. In the realm of fashion, this means embracing more sustainable and minimalist practices.

The fashion industry has long been associated with excess and waste, with the fast fashion model encouraging consumers to constantly buy new clothing, only to discard it a few months later. But as we become more aware of the impact of this on the environment and on workers in the fashion industry, there is a growing movement towards more mindful consumption.

In the coming years, we can expect to see a greater emphasis on sustainable and ethical fashion, with designers and retailers alike working to reduce their environmental footprint and improve working conditions for those in the industry. This includes using more sustainable materials, reducing waste, and promoting fair labor practices.

At the same time, the minimalist approach to fashion is likely to continue to gain traction, as people seek to simplify their lives and reduce clutter. The capsule wardrobe, with its emphasis on a few high-quality pieces that can be mixed and matched, is a perfect example of this trend.

As we look to the future, it is important to remember that our clothing choices have the power to shape the world around us. By embracing a minimalist approach to fashion, we can reduce our impact on the environment and make a positive difference in the lives of those who make our clothing.

Personally, I have seen the benefits of adopting a more minimalist approach to fashion. By focusing on quality over quantity and choosing versatile pieces that can be worn in multiple ways, I have been able to reduce my wardrobe while still feeling stylish and put together. And by choosing more sustainable and ethical options, I feel good about the impact of my choices.

In the end, the future of fashion is in our hands. By embracing a more minimalist and sustainable approach, we can create a better world for ourselves and for future generations.

Conclusion

As we near the end of this book on minimalism and clothing, I hope you have found the information provided useful and thought-provoking.

I've shared with you the philosophy of minimalism, the benefits of a minimalist wardrobe, and the various ways in which you can build and curate your own minimalist closet.

Throughout this journey, I have stressed the importance of understanding your personal style, investing in quality pieces, and making choices that reflect your values and goals.

Minimalism is not a one-size-fits-all solution, but a mindset and lifestyle that can be adapted to suit your individual needs and circumstances. It's about living with intention and purpose, and finding joy in the things that truly matter to you.

As for me, I can attest to the transformative power of minimalism. It has allowed me to focus on the things that truly matter in my life, to let go of excess, and to live more intentionally.

Of course, I am not perfect, and I still struggle with the allure of consumerism and the desire for more. However, I am committed to the journey and the ongoing process of simplifying and streamlining my life.

I hope this book has inspired you to take your own steps towards minimalism and to see the potential for transformation that exists in the simple act of decluttering and streamlining your wardrobe.

As we move forward, I encourage you to continue exploring the world of minimalism and to find what works best for you. Remember that minimalism is not about deprivation, but about making intentional choices and finding true joy and fulfillment in the things that matter most.

Thank you for joining me on this journey. Here's to a more intentional and purposeful life.

Dear Reader,

Thank you for embarking on this journey with me and delving into the world of minimalism and fashion. I hope that this book has been enlightening and inspiring, and that you have gained valuable insights into how a minimalist wardrobe can transform your life.

It has been an absolute pleasure to share my knowledge and experience with you, and I would be honored if you would consider leaving a positive review. Your feedback helps me to continue to improve my writing and bring more meaningful content to readers like you.

Thank you once again for taking the time to read this book. I hope that you continue to explore the benefits of minimalism and fashion, and that they enhance your life in ways you never imagined.

Yours sincerely,

Hazel

Printed in Great Britain
by Amazon